My Life
of
MIRACLES

As you read this book my friend Ninfa wrote, I pray you will look and see miracles God made in your life

Teresa Balderas

NINFA (BENJI) OLMSTEAD

ISBN 978-1-64349-692-4 (paperback)
ISBN 978-1-64349-693-1 (digital)

Copyright © 2020 by Ninfa (Benji) Olmstead

All rights reserved. No part of this publication may be reproduced, distributed, or transmitted in any form or by any means, including photocopying, recording, or other electronic or mechanical methods without the prior written permission of the publisher. For permission requests, solicit the publisher via the address below.

Christian Faith Publishing, Inc.
832 Park Avenue
Meadville, PA 16335
www.christianfaithpublishing.com

Printed in the United States of America

I was brought into this world some years ago, and since that day, God has had his eyes and hands on me. So on my very first birthday came my first grand healing miracle. As I was growing up, my mother told me that before my first birthday, I got sick with a stroke. I was paralyzed, and it was only one side of my body, and it was for three days. But on the day of my first birthday, my mother told me that I picked up my hand that was paralyzed to pick up my baby's bottle to drink. So there was my first healing miracle that God did in me. Everything was doing great and wonderful as my life continued. But then later on, here came the enemy again. I was at the age of eight, and we would walk to school, me and my brothers and sisters. So one day when we were walking home, we were getting ready to cross a road. I saw a motorcycle coming down the road. I guess I thought I was going to make it across the road, but I didn't make it in crossing the road. I was run over by the motorcycle.

And then after it happened, I was taken home by the police. So I guess that meant that I didn't get hurt, so I thank God 'cause he was there for me again, 'cause he is so good all the time. So my life continued; then later on, there came the enemy again. It was a cold evening night, and I was still at the age of eight. I was warming myself up in front of the old-fashioned heaters. I had a sleeping dress on, so as I was standing there, my dress was caught on fire. And one good thing about it was that my dad was lying down on the sofa. He saw me, and he got up real quick and threw a blanket on me to stop the fire on my dress. God was there with me again. I burned up one of my legs, and it took three weeks to get better for me to be able to go back to school, but the part I liked was that I didn't go to school for three weeks, so my life continued on ahead. So here came another day when God was there with me again.

I was still young, so we had an outside house. I guess I was clumsy; I decided to get on top of the outside house. And I decided to jump down from it, and as I jumped down, one of my feet got hurt because there was a big nail on the ground. So when my foot hit the ground, a nail went inside my foot, but thank God that my foot got better later on. Another time that God was watching over me was when I had to wash the dishes, and it was on big pots. I finished washing the dishes, and we had to throw the water away after finishing the dishes, and it was a strong pouring rainy day. So as I went out to throw the water, I stretched out my arms; but as I was throwing it away, I fell off the porch. So that means that I went along with the pot of water, and I fell in a big mud puddle. But I thank God that I didn't break a bone when I fell down.

I continued going on and on with my life, so at the age of eighteen, it was the time that I gave my life to God. This was the time when the enemy started with me because there came an illness into my life. It was the illness of seizures, so my family took me to go see a lot of special doctors, but they really couldn't find out the reason on how they started, but I knew that God was with me anyway, no matter what I would go through. I was still working in different jobs when I was having the seizures, and on one of the jobs that I worked in, I got fired, and my oldest sister—she was working there also—decided to quit from there. It was maybe 'cause I was fired, so I continued, and then later on, I still continued working. I started another job, but it seemed that the illness started getting a little worse on me, so I decided just to quit working because I knew that my parents were worried because I was driving by myself every day, and it was out of town also.

But I still kept on doing the Lord's will, and another day came where we lived in a two-story house, and the porches were very high. I was sitting on the porch. I had a seizure, and I fell off the porch. It was on my back that fell into a lot of bushes that were behind me; I thank God because he was there for me again. All that I got were just bruises and scratches on me; I didn't break a bone. Another day,

I was in church. It was a youth service, so as I was leading the service, there came the enemy in me having a seizure while being behind the pulpit, but the Lord helped me there again. So I still continued seeing the doctors.

Another day later on, I was ironing clothes; so as I was doing it, I had a seizure, and the iron fell down on top of my foot. I didn't feel the pain until the blackout was over with, so the iron was very hot that it left my middle toes stuck with each other. For a whole year, I couldn't wear a shoe on that foot, so I thank God 'cause he was there watching over me again. As I was going through all this, I decided to do something that I would enjoy doing. One thing that I love is music and singing to the Lord. So I decided to become a volunteer singer at a youth center 'cause as I was listening to a radio program, there was a chaplain talking with the DJ/radioman, and he was saying if anybody that was listening to the radio and they would like to go speak or sing to the youth, just to call them. So I called, and they invited me. So I was going there like every two or three months here, and then later on, the chaplain began a good friend of mine.

So he told me that I should go try to be a volunteer singer at the nursing homes also. So I did call. Since 1992, I started going to one of them, and I'm still going there as of today. They already gave me a name there, and the name is "Superstar Benji," and the part of Benji was given to me from a great friend that God blessed me for a couple of years until he went home to the Lord. He told me that it was mentioned in God's book as Benjamin as a brave soldier 'cause my friend would tell me that I was very brave in fighting the illness of seizures. So that's why I told them at the nursing home to add that name with the one they had given there from them. And I also cut it short that name that my friend gave me into Benji. Later on, as I continued going on and on, I was still seeing my doctors. One day I went to see him, and he spoke to me about a surgery, so I decided to go through it. It was surgery on my brain, but it really didn't help the seizures. All it did was that it gave me a lot of memory loss, so sometimes people talk to me of things that have happened in the past, but I tell them that I don't remember, so they try to remind me, but it was still hard for me to remember. But I still continued through my journey.

About four months later after that surgery, I got real sick with another one. As I was washing the dishes, I had a strong one, and my hand was on the hot water, but I couldn't feel anything because of the blackout I was having. They called 911, and my parents told them to check the temperature of the water, and they said that it was 130 degrees. I was taken to the hospital, and they tried doing their best in helping me, but they really couldn't, so they flew me to Dallas, Texas, where they had special doctors for burns. As I was there, my parents told me that they felt hurt in seeing me in the way that I looked, and I also had three weeks of amnesia. That's why I can't remember anything about it. And some close friends of mine also told me that they went over to see me there. But I told them that I couldn't remember anything about it. And the doctors also had to do skin graft on my hand 'cause all the fingers were also stuck together, so they had to do a surgery in separating the fingers. All I could see on my hand was mostly all the staples that they put on it. After being in the hospital, I was released from there, and I was brought home, and it was the season of Christmas. The day that my family got together at my parents' home, I was happy to be there, and I tell people today that I guess I was good for that year because I received a couple of gifts there. Then I also thought it was because I was barely released from the hospital because today now when Christmas comes, I don't get anything, but I'm still happy when that special day gets here.

I continued through my journey, and there was only one brave one in the family to be able to change my patches every day, and that was Marissa. So then later on, I decided to go to therapy so I could use my hand again. When I started doing the exercise there, they brought me a handgripper to start doing exercise with, and me and my hand didn't like it 'cause it would hurt a lot. And I even named him Miky. I told the therapist that me and Miky did not get along with each other 'cause every time that my hand would squeeze it, my hand would really hurt. After going there for six months, I thank God because I was able to use my hand again. I started writing again, and it started out in me.

Writing like a first grader writes, I was able to use again my hand also in playing the keyboard and also to make a fist, and that was the goal that my doctor had told me to do. I went to show my doctor my hand, and I also was making a fist, showing him, and he was so happy to see it. And also in therapy, they gave me a certificate there and guess who they put in there? Well, it was a picture of Miky, the one I didn't like. But that was sweet of them, so I was so thankful to God because he was still there for me, and he kept on giving me more and more strength every day. I continued telling people that no matter what we would go through in our lives, we have to keep on 'cause there's something good waiting for us at the end of our journey. The years kept going on and on, and I was so thankful because I was doing and feeling so much better with the seizures.

After a year or two, I passed without having a seizure. I spoke to my parents that I would love to drive again 'cause I had to stop for a while in driving. They really didn't want for me to drive, but I still decided to get a car. So I bought one from one of my sisters. At the beginning, everything was going on real good with me 'cause I was driving again, and I was very happy for that, but this enemy had to come back to bug me 'cause as I was driving on the highway on my own, I had a seizure again. Yes, they came back again, so as I was having it, I was getting a blackout while I was driving. My car went to the side of the highway, and my car was all destroyed. I even hit a sign that was there, but I thank God that he was there watching over me 'cause I didn't get hurt, so it meant that it wasn't my time yet to go home. So after that, my family wanted me to stop driving, so I stopped doing that.

My life still continued serving the Lord, so then later on, it was the day of Fourth of July. I decided to cook something, so I was there standing front of the stove. I had a seizure, and one of my hands was put on the burner, and it stayed there for a while because I was having a blackout, and I didn't feel it until after the blackout was over with. It was hurting a lot, so they took me to ER, and they had to cut off my wedding rings because my fingers got very swollen. I had to have a surgery on my fingers, so I tell people that I guess I was a firecracker on that day because it happened on Fourth of July. I continued through my journey, and also I used to enjoy playing volleyball with my family on Sundays, but I told them that I couldn't play anymore because of my hands; then later on, I decided to have another surgery.

And I barely met my husband-to-be. It was barely three weeks of knowing him, so they put a VNS wire in me to help me with the seizures. One thing that happened was that it did help a little because I can feel it now when one is coming, but the other thing I didn't like was because they destroyed one of my vocal chords, and I'm a person that loves to sing. But I thank God that he helps me in being able to sing his Word to elderlies at the nursing homes and in the church also. After a while, a couple of months later, I was traveling with my family, and it had been about seven or eight months that I was having trouble with both of my knees, and I was also using a cane to walk. As I was coming back home, I was sitting in a third seat in a van, and I didn't have my seat belt on. We were in an accident, and I went to hit with my knees on the seat that was in front of me, and my knees hit real hard on that seat. Thank God that nobody got hurt in that accident, and here came my precious Lord again with another healing miracle because three or four days later, I was walking without the cane, and I was so happy. I even went to go see the doctor, and I told him and I showed him that God did a miracle on my knees. I told him that I didn't need the surgery anymore, and he was surprised and happy for me.

Now a couple of years passed by, and then another grand healing miracle came for me. It was the time of thanksgiving, and I come from a big family. But on this day, it was a little sad because not everybody showed up, and some of them weren't even speaking with each other, so only a few showed up there at my dad's house on that day. On that Monday following that holiday, there came the enemy again. I had a seizure there at my dad's house. I was sitting on a chair on the dining room, and I fell back from the chair, and I hit my head on some bricks. They took me to ER, so for four days, I had amnesia. I didn't remember what happened to me. Then on the fifth day, I started coming back, and I started remembering where I was and who I was also. In the evening, I told my husband for us to go visit the neighbors across the street, so we went up there. Then after a while of being there, I started feeling something on my ankles. It was moving up, so I told my husband to take me home. As I got there, my dad came over to me. I told him that I felt that my time was coming for me to go home and rest with the Lord, and he said, "No, it can't be." But I told him that it was, so they called 911, and they took me.

As I was in there in the ambulance, I remember hearing the paramedic telling the driver that they had lost me, that I was gone already. And my husband told me that he was following the ambulance, and he said that they had turned off the flashing lights from the ambulance. So as the paramedic said those words, I've been telling so many people on what happened to me. I saw the beautiful sky opening up, and I saw my beloved mom there and some other elderlies that have gone home also. And then a great, wonderful voice told me these words: "I have a place prepared for you here, but it's not your time yet, so I'm sending you back down to tell my people to get prepared because I am coming very soon." After this the next thing, I remember was that it was the following day, and I was at home, and I thank God that my family was there around my bed, where I was lying down. So I thank God that he put my family back together again.

I really have been telling a lot of people about these special words that were given to me to tell them, and now I thank my Lord for helping me and for being here with me. So now me and my husband decided to move out from my dad's house to start our own lives. We moved out on our own to a small town, and I even became a volunteer singer at that town's nursing home also. And I thank God 'cause we were so happy, and we were doing very well and feeling better. But the enemy was still around, and I know that 'cause that's the way he is with God's children everywhere. And if I happen to have a seizure today, I can feel them coming, and they are very light, compared to the ones that I used to have in the past. Today I tell people that we are in peace now, and we are very happy also, and even our neighbor is happy to have us here. She tells her family and friends that me and my husband are her angels, and I thank God for that.

These are just some of the miracles that I can remember because of memory loss from one of the surgeries I had, but I know that God has done so many other miracles in me. All you have to do is just believe and trust in him. This is what I leave you: it's to trust in the Lord with all your heart and lean not on your own understanding (Proverbs 3:5). So now I sing because I am very happy, but I know that the enemy will still be around until the coming of our Lord. But all we got to do is to hold on to his hand because our God can help us through an illness. Because I am one of them that he has helped, and our Lord will give us the power to fight the enemy, and I am still fighting these seizures. But our Lord is still there with me, and he is my Protector. So he will always be there for you also because God has no favorite. He loves us all still the same.

And today I am so thankful to my Lord because so many tell me when they see me that I have been a strong child of God. From everything that I have gone through 'cause of this illness, but I thank my precious Lord for that. So what I tell them is just to believe and trust in God always 'cause he will always be there for us and with us. I just want to keep on doing his will, no matter what I will go through in my life because I want to go see my precious Lord face-to-face to thank him for everything that he did for me and for everything that he is doing for me and for everything that he's going to do for me, and of course, to go see all my loved ones that have gone also.

Also, once there was a friend of mine named Letecia Gamez whom I was talking to about my life in me having all these accidents that I went through in getting burned from this illness of mine. She told me that the reason I was getting burned was because I was gonna be on fire for Jesus, and I thank God for that. Our Lord is the one that gives us the strength every day, so what we all need to do is to just take one day at a time, to continue through our journey. Remember that he loves you because he is nothing but love, and if you would like to go to heaven, all I say to you is to call this number, which is 1-800-252-LORD. Okay, and they gonna tell about it, and also, you'll be able to talk with a great, wonderful Christian friend of mine who is Patsy Jo James. She is the president of Gotel Ministries, and I'm an advisory board member from it. But they will be there to help you and also pray for you. To write these testimonies of my life. It was a great Christian friend of mine—her name is Teresa Balderas—

who talked me into telling the people of my life of miracles, and I also want to thank God for every person that helped me through all those years when I was going through all those strong seizures. There was my family. My dad is named Abel Robles Sr., and my late mom was named Delfina Robles. Then my seven brothers and my six sisters were also there to help me, but now God blessed me with a great and wonderful husband named Norman Olmstead. Now he is there by my side watching over me, so this means that God can grant any miracle for us 'cause if he did it for me, he'll also do it for you because our Lord is everywhere, and he has his arms open wide for you also. I also tell the people today that I am very thankful and very happy because, in the past, I was mainly in the hospital and also in ambulances, but not anymore today. Today I just go for a checkup every six months, and I thank God because my doctor tells me that I am doing good. It's because of God.

God is continuing in blessing and healing and still doing miracles in me. In the beginning of 2018, we started going to classes to be able to be foster parents and then adopt. Praise God that we completed in doing everything that we were supposed to do. So now, we have the license to do that already. So me, and my husband are so happy for that, but the enemy didn't like it that I was so happy that he came to bug me again, I was bitten by a spider but my Lord was still there for me because I had to go through a surgery cause by the infection was deep. But I thank God that he helped me again and I was also thankful for my loving husband because he was there in changing my patch every night for six weeks. And now I am very thankful in continuing in being a blessing to people, I know that it's because of God not me because this past summer my pocket phone ran out of batteries and card also.

So I told my husband to buy me a card for it, so he went and he did buy me a card and he also brought a bigger phone also, I wasn't expecting that, but I knew that it was my Lord that did that, because there has been a lot of years that I have been writing messages from preachers and ministers, I feel that it was God that told my husband to buy that because it was time for me to open up that book, to spread Gods word to everyone and I didn't even know anything about Facebook and then to send them out also but God showed me how to do it, so now every morning I get up and send out a message to people, it was the month of August, I want to thank God that the messages has blessed a lot of people, they text me and tell me that they enjoy the messages and some people tell me that they can't wait for the next day to see the next message and I am so thankful to God for that. In September it was our anniversary and my husband's birthday and I didn't know how but there came God again in helping me because on that day before. We went to my husband's cousin Teresa, she and her partner were able to show me in how to do it. See how God is so good all the time, he'll be there for us and on that year of 2018, God blessed my family more because four of my nieces had babies. So, my family grew more. And I know that my mom and my sister Minnie would've enjoyed seeing that especially on the holidays, but I know that mom and Minnie are very happy where they are at right now in Heaven, on Christmas of 2018. I went to one of the nursing homes to sing some songs. We enjoyed it because we had a Mrs. Claus with us and all the elderly's enjoyed that. So that's why I also wanted to write this book, to let all of you all know that my life of miracles has been sometimes hard and sometimes easy but it's all because of God that I am still around today and God is the only one that you can count on, until our precious Lord returns to come take us home because if you happen to give up, just remember that it's not going to be easy for you just remember that nothing is impossible for our Lord to heal us from and he can remove anything away from us also may God bless each and every person that has read this book in my life of miracles.

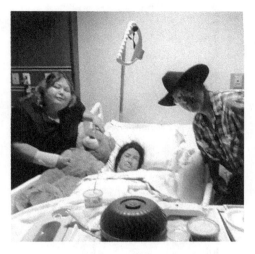

We were visiting my husband's sister in Oklahoma Hospital, then about 2 weeks later she went to Heaven

A picture that me and my husband took on Christmas 2018

That's me with Mr and Mrs Claus at the nursing home

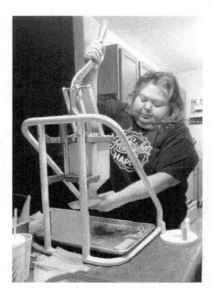

That's me making tameles, with the new style of today, it was in December 2018

Me and my husband enjoying Thanksgiving
with his family in 2018

Me and Santa Claus at the nursing home where
I sing on Christmas season in 2018

I'm on my way to go to the first Sunday service to my church in 2019

Me and my Dad on the night of Christmas Eve in 2018

This is my newest picture, so this is how happy I am feeling today

This is my friend Teresa whom talked
me into writing about miracles

These are my friends Patsy Jo James from Gotel ministries, and her belated husband Randy James, whom gave me the name Benji

My long time friend Leticia Gamez whom told me that I got burned because I was gonna be on fire for Jesus

My niece Marissa whom was brave enough to change my patches when I burned my hand

Here with my Dad whom was celebrating one of his birthday

Sitting at the chair of the president of Gotel ministries

Me celebrating one of my birthdays with
my Dad and my belated Mom

Me and my husband before we got married

Me and my husband leaving for our honeymoon

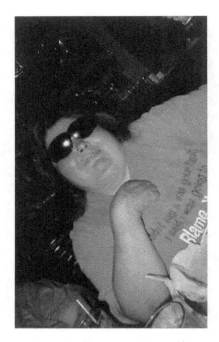

Me enjoying myself at a restaurant with my Mon and my sisterss

Me with my great friend Patsy Jo James president of Gotel ministries and a belated friend from that ministries

Me and my husband with one of my brothers,
and friends from California

My Wedding Day

Me and my husband with Santa Claus

Me resting at home

Here with Santa Claus at a Nursing Home

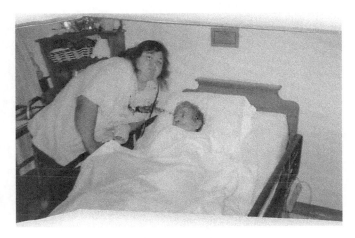

Here with my belated Mother-in-laws at a Nursing Home

Here with my parents 50th Anniversary with my brothers and sisters, and there is still one brother and one sister that didn't come out, Mom had 7 boys & 7 girls

We are in Corpus Chriti, Tx and my hands were still wrapped up from the burns

We are in Oklahoma on my husbands vacation

Here with the Chaplains from Waco Center For Youth in Waco, Tx and he helped me to become a volunteer at a nursing home

Our Wedding Day

Here with some pastors from Mexico my
church went to a missionary

We are here with my Dad on Fathers Day

The day my husband proposed to me

We took a picture with our pastors at our church

Me singing as usaul at my church

ABOUT THE AUTHOR

People have told Ninfa (Benji) Olmstead that she has been a great servant of the Lord. They said that she has been a big fighter against the enemy, even though she has suffered in so many years. Some have told her that she has been a good example to them. She thanks God for that, and then others have told her that she has blessed so much with the songs that she praises God with. She enjoys singing to the elderlies at the nursing homes also. She will continue doing the best for her Lord.

CPSIA information can be obtained
at www.ICGtesting.com
Printed in the USA
LVHW091044100820
662812LV00001B/266